Sports Illustrated KIDS

STATS AND STORIES

FOOTBALL STATS AND THE STORIES BEHIND THEM

What Every Fan Needs to Know

by Shane Frederick

CAPSTONE PRESS
a capstone imprint

Sports Illustrated Kids Stats & Stories are published by Capstone Press,
1710 Roe Crest Drive, North Mankato, Minnesota 56003.
www.mycapstone.com

Library of Congress Cataloging-in-Publication Data
is available on the Library of Congress website.
ISBN 978-1-4914-8214-8 (library binding)
ISBN 978-1-4914-8583-5 (paperback)
ISBN 978-1-4914-8587-3 (eBook PDF)

Editorial Credits
Nick Healy, editor; Ted Williams, designer; Eric Gohl, media researcher;
Tori Abraham, production specialist

Photo Credits
AP Photo: NFL Photos, 18; Getty Images: Christian Petersen, 37; Newscom: Ai Wire
Photo Service/David Greene, 40; Sports Illustrated: Al Tielemans, 13, 19, 23, 29, 30,
31, 39, 41, Andy Hayt, 20, 44 (top), Damian Strohmeyer, 12, David E. Klutho, 43, John
Biever, 5, 14–15, 45, John Iacono, 27, John W. McDonough, 17, 24, 44 (bottom), Manny
Millan, 7, Robert Beck, 6, 32, 34, 42, Simon Bruty, cover, 1, 9, 11

Editor's Note
All statistics are through the 2014 NFL season unless otherwise noted.

Printed in the United States of America in North Mankato, Minnesota.
112015   009221CGS16

TABLE OF CONTENTS

STATS ON THE FIELD

On an October day in 1920, the Dayton Triangles took on the Columbus Panhandles in what is considered the first game in what fans now know as the National Football League (NFL). Although no highlight reel from that day exists, the contest lives on in numbers.

During the game, which the Triangles won 14-0, Al Mahrt tossed a 30-yard pass to Dutch Thiele. Lou Partlow ran 7 yards for a touchdown, and Frank Bacon scampered 60 yards on a punt return for a score. George Kinderdine kicked two extra points. Those statistics were noted, recorded, and preserved, reminding us of what happened that day in Dayton, Ohio.

Statistics are the numbers that tell the story of games, seasons, eras, and careers. The game of football has changed over the years, but statistics allow us to compare players and contrast styles. In 1932, for instance, Green Bay Packers quarterback Arnie Herber led the league with 639 passing yards in 14 games. In 2014, the New Orleans Saints' Drew Brees led the way, slinging the ball for 4,952 yards, playing in just two more games.

At the same time, the record for touchdown passes in one game—seven—is shared by players from different eras: Brees in 2015, Nick Foles of the Philadelphia Eagles and Peyton Manning of the Denver Broncos in 2013, Joe Kapp of the Minnesota Vikings in 1969, Y.A. Tittle of the New York Giants in 1962, George Blanda of the Houston Oilers in 1961, Adrian Burk of the Eagles in 1954, and Sid Luckman of the Chicago Bears in 1943.

Over time, more and more statistics have been added to better explain and analyze the sport, from quarterback rating in the 1970s to quarterback sacks in the 1980s to the probability of success on certain plays in more recent years. So fasten your chinstrap and get ready to crunch the numbers. You're about to find out about the players behind the numbers, how they reached those marks, and precisely what these stats mean.

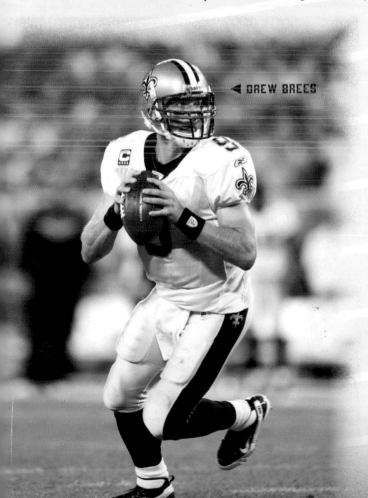

◄ DREW BREES

CHAPTER 1
THE PASSING GAME

Star quarterbacks are the face of the NFL. From Tom Brady to Russell Wilson to Aaron Rodgers, the quarterbacks run the show with their leadership skills and cannon arms. Every season, it seems, passing becomes a bigger, more important part of the game. Over time, the number of attempted passes has risen, and the accuracy of the quarterbacks has improved as well.

Passing accuracy is measured in completion percentage. That number is calculated by dividing the number of completed passes by the number of attempts. For example, in 2014 the New Orleans Saints' Drew Brees completed 456 of 659 passes for a 69.2 completion percentage.

$$456 \div 659 = .692 \ \text{(or 69.2 percent)}$$

▶ RUSSELL WILSON

The passing game has exploded in modern-day football. Rule changes have played a part. The NFL tightened rules to protect quarterbacks from vicious hits. The league also expanded limits on defensive backs' contact with receivers. Strategy has changed, too. In 2014 NFL quarterbacks completed 62.6 percent of their passes. Ten years earlier that number was 59.8 percent. Thirty years earlier it was 56.4—and teams attempted an average of 47 fewer passes per season back then. Back in 1940 it was 42.9 percent.

BEST SINGLE-SEASON COMPLETION PERCENTAGES

Rank	Player	Team	%	Year
1.	DREW BREES	SAINTS	71.2%	2011
2.	DREW BREES	SAINTS	70.6%	2009
	KEN ANDERSON	BENGALS	70.6%	1982
4.	STEVE YOUNG	49ERS	70.3%	1994
5.	JOE MONTANA	49ERS	70.2%	1989

▶ STEVE YOUNG

A FORMULA FOR GREATNESS

Completion percentage isn't the only way to measure a quarterback's success. Coaches, players, and fans also pay close attention to passing yards, touchdown passes, and interceptions. But is there one stat that sums up a quarterback's performance?

In the early 1970s, a complex formula was created to do just that. The new stat was dubbed the passer rating. It uses a quarterback's most important passing numbers to arrive at one stat.

To find a quarterback's passer rating, you need the following numbers: passes completed, passes attempted, passing yards, passing touchdowns, and interceptions. Equipped with those pieces of information and a calculator, follow these steps:

1. Divide the QB's completed passes by attempts.
2. Subtract 0.3.
3. Multiply that number by 5 and record the result (product).
4. Divide passing yards by pass attempts.
5. Subtract 3.
6. Divide that number by 4 and record the result (quotient).
7. Divide touchdown passes by pass attempts.
8. Multiply that number by 20 and record the result (product).
9. Divide interceptions by pass attempts.
10. Multiply that number by 25.
11. Subtract that number from 2.375 and record the result (difference).
12. Add the numbers you recorded after steps 3, 6, 8, and 11.

(Note: The result at each of those steps cannot be greater than 2.375 or less than zero. If they are, award 2.375 as a maximum or zero as a minimum.)

13. Multiply that sum by 100.
14. Divide that number by 6.
15. The final result is the passer rating.

The passer rating is difficult to calculate, but it's easy to understand. A passer rating over 100 is terrific. A number in the 90s is very good. A passer rating in the 80s is fair, and below 80 is poor. In 2014, Tony Romo of the Dallas Cowboys led the NFL with a passer rating of 113.2. Jacksonville Jaguars rookie Blake Bortels finished with the league's worst passer rating at 69.5.

Aaron Rodgers of the Green Bay Packers set the record for passer rating in a single season in 2011. He attempted 502 passes and completed 343. He threw for 4,643 yards, with 45 touchdown passes and only 6 interceptions. His passer rating was 122.5.

After the season, Rodgers won his first Most Valuable Player (MVP) award, having led his Packers to a 15-1 record.

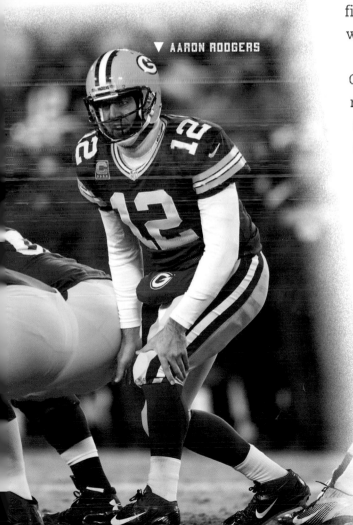

▼ AARON RODGERS

PICKED OFF

Clearly the best thing a quarterback can do for his team is throw a touchdown pass. The worst thing he can do is throw an interception. The best quarterbacks throw far more touchdowns than interceptions.

Comparing these two kinds of plays results in a statistic called the touchdown-to-interception ratio. It is calculated by dividing the passer's touchdowns by interceptions.

In 2013, the Broncos' Peyton Manning threw an NFL-record 55 touchdown passes. He also tossed 10 balls to the other team. That gave him a 5.5 touchdown-to-interception ratio. For every interception he tossed that season, he threw 5.5 touchdown passes.

The best single-season ratio belonged to the Eagles' Nick Foles, who threw 27 touchdowns passes and just two interceptions for a 13.5 ratio. That also took place in 2013. While Foles played well and didn't make costly mistakes that season, he wasn't as dynamic as Manning, who won his fifth MVP award after that season.

MOST INTERCEPTIONS IN A SINGLE SEASON

Rank	Player	Team	Interceptions	Year
1.	GEORGE BLANDA	OILERS	42	1962
2.	VINNY TESTAVERDE	BUCCANEERS	35	1988
3.	FRANK TRIPUCKA	BRONCOS	34	1960
4.	JOHN HADL	CHARGERS	32	1968
	FRAN TARKENTON	VIKINGS	32	1978

Fifty years earlier, New York Giants quarterback Y.A. Tittle was the MVP. He led the NFL with 36 touchdown passes. But in an era when teams didn't throw as much as they do today and when there was a little more tolerance for turnovers, Tittle also tossed 14 interceptions. That was one pick for every 2.57 scoring strikes.

◀ PEYTON MANNING

CHAPTER 2

RECEIVING

If a quarterback is going to have success, he needs to have some teammates who can haul in his passes, whether they're quick slants and outs or deep posts and bombs. In 2002 Marvin Harrison was Peyton Manning's most-trusted receiver. He caught an NFL-record 143 passes for the Indianapolis Colts that season.

MOST RECEPTIONS, CAREER

Rank	Player	Team	Receptions
1.	JERRY RICE	49ERS/RAIDERS/SEAHAWKS	1,549
2.	TONY GONZALEZ	CHIEFS/FALCONS	1,325
3.	MARVIN HARRISON	COLTS	1,102
4.	CRIS CARTER	EAGLES/VIKINGS/DOLPHINS	1,101
5.	TIM BROWN	RAIDERS/BUCCANEERS	1,094

▶ MARVIN HARRISON

But what happened immediately after each of those 143 receptions? That can be the real highlight of the game.

Official passing and receiving yards are measurements of entire plays. They reflect the total distance from the line of scrimmage until the receiver is tackled, goes out of bounds, or scores. But a stat called yards after the catch (YAC) gives credit to the receiver for what he does after securing the ball. That may include breaking tackles or outrunning defenders to get extra yards. Each receiver's YAC are measured by statisticians as a separate number. To get YAC, simply subtract the yards the ball travels through the air from the total number of receiving yards.

In 2014 Bears running back Matt Forte racked up 771 of his 808 receiving yards after catching passes. He caught 102 balls, grabbing many of them on screen passes or other passes around or even behind the line of scrimmage.

▶ MATT FORTE

GOING THE DISTANCE

Nine different quarterback-receiver combinations have hooked up for 99-yard touchdown passes. How many yards covered in those plays were YAC? Check out these examples:

◀ VICTOR CRUZ

- In 2011, the Patriots' Wes Welker caught Tom Brady's 17-yard pass, broke a tackle, and ran 82 yards for a score.

- Also in 2011, the Giants' Victor Cruz grabbed Eli Manning's 10-yard pass and broke three tackles as he ran the remaining 89 yards.

- In 2008, the Vikings' Bernard Berrian was wide open as he caught a 45-yard bomb from Gus Frerotte and sprinted 54 yards for the touchdown.

- In 1995, the Packers' Robert Brooks hauled in a Brett Favre pass of 29 yards and ran 70 yards to pay dirt.

MOST CATCHES IN A GAME

Rank	Player	Team	Catches	Year
1.	BRANDON MARSHALL	BRONCOS	21	2009
2.	TERRELL OWENS	49ERS	20	2000
3.	TOM FEARS	RAMS	18	1950
3.	JASON WITTEN	COWBOYS	18	2012
3.	BRANDON MARSHALL	BRONCOS	18	2008

HANG ON TIGHT

Receivers are some of the most athletic players in the game. They need to be able to run fast, cut quick, and jump high. But more importantly, they need to be sure-handed. Teams and other observers keep track of the number of times a receiver drops a pass as well as the number of times that player is targeted on a play.

In 2014 three receivers were blamed for the most dropped passes with 10 each: the Panthers' Kelvin Benjamin, the Ravens' Steve Smith, and the Broncos' Demaryius Thomas. The drops weren't so bad for Thomas, who was targeted a league-leading 184 times and made 111 catches, which ranked second in the league. The Steelers' Antonio Brown led the NFL with 129 receptions and had just five drops.

The most reliable receiver that season might have been Cowboys running back DeMarco Murray. He was targeted 64 times and caught 57 passes (89.1 percent) with only one drop. The other six passes were defended or considered uncatchable.

◄ DEMARYIUS THOMAS

CHAPTER 3
THE RUNNING GAME

◀ BEATTIE FEATHERS

Running backs may not be the glamour boys they used to be, but they're still the workhorses, plowing through the lines to try to gain tough yards. Running backs' prowess is measured in the total yards they gain each down, game, and season, and over their entire careers.

Since the Chicago Bears' Beattie Feathers rushed for 1,004 yards in 11 games in 1934, the 1,000-yard threshold has been a standard many backs strive to reach. Plenty of backs have accomplished that, although it took 13 years after Feathers for the next runner to hit that mark. That was Steve Van Buren of the Philadelphia Eagles, who had 1,008 yards in 12 games. The 1,500-yard milestone has been achieved 86 times, while 2,000 yards has been hit just seven times. Those totals have been helped by the NFL's adding games to its season, going to 14 in 1961 and 16 in 1978.

2,000-YARD SEASONS

Rank	Player	Team	Yards	Year
1.	ERIC DICKERSON	RAMS	2,105	1984
2.	ADRIAN PETERSON	VIKINGS	2,097	2012
3.	JAMAL LEWIS	RAVENS	2,066	2003
4.	BARRY SANDERS	LIONS	2,053	1997
5.	TERRELL DAVIS	BRONCOS	2,008	1998
6.	CHRIS JOHNSON	TITANS	2,006	2009
7.	O.J. SIMPSON	BILLS	2,003	1973

▶ JAMAL LEWIS

► ERIC DICKERSON

PLAY BY PLAY

In one of the most-impressive rushing performances in recent history, the Minnesota Vikings' Adrian Peterson in 2012 fell just 8 yards shy of Eric Dickerson's single-season record of 2,105 yards. Peterson needed to gain 208 yards on the final day of the regular season to break the record. He finished with a still-impressive 199 yards to help his team make the playoffs.

Comparing the two seasons, Peterson carried the ball 348 times to average 6.0 yards per carry. He also averaged 131.1 yards per game. Dickerson had 379 rushes for a 5.6-yard average. He averaged 131.6 yards per game. Their yards per game ranked fourth and fifth all-time. The Buffalo Bills' O.J. Simpson holds the record with 143.1 yards per game in 1973, when he ran 2,003 yards in 14 games. That's two fewer games than Peterson and Dickerson played.

Perhaps a better way to judge a running back's talents is by measuring yards per attempt. Take the player's total yards and divide by the number of carries. Beattie Feathers still holds the yards-per-carry record with 8.4 during that 1934 season. It's been matched once, however. Falcons quarterback Michael Vick averaged that number in 2006, rushing 123 times for 1,039 yards.

TOUGH TO TAKE DOWN

Running backs who are tough to tackle are valuable to teams. While they rely on offensive linemen and other teammates to open holes and create running lanes with sturdy blocks, ball carriers have to put in their own work, too. A runner who can bounce off defenders and break tackles is more valuable than one who is easily tripped up. In recent years, observers have begun counting the yards gained after a back has been first contacted by a defensive player.

The Seattle Seahawks' Marshawn Lynch does that better than anyone as he goes into his trademarked "Beast Mode." In 2014 he averaged 2.53 yards after first contact on each rushing attempt. During a 2011 playoff game against the New Orleans Saints, Lynch blasted through the line and ran 67 yards for a touchdown. Along the way, he broke, pushed, shoved, and ran away from eight missed tackles.

◀ MARSHAWN LYNCH

THE TD SPECIALIST

In 1998, his final season as a pro, Detroit Lions great Barry Sanders rushed for 1,491 yards. But he scored just four touchdowns that season. His lead blocker, fullback "Touchdown" Tommy Vardell, scored six TDs, despite rushing for only 37 yards that season.

CHAPTER 4

THE SPECIALISTS

Football seems to get more and more specialized every year, with five-receiver formations, third-down running backs, and even kickers who handle only kickoffs (and not field goals or punts). There is a stat, however, for the players who do it all. All-purpose yardage adds together rushing, receiving, kick return, and punt return yards.

The great San Francisco 49ers wide receiver Jerry Rice holds the all-time record for all-purpose yards with 23,546. The vast majority of those yards were receiving yards, though. He had only 645 rushing yards over his 20-year career and returned six kickoffs and no punts. Not far behind in second place is Brian Mitchell, who was truly an all-purpose player for the Washington Redskins and two others teams. His 23,330 yards were divided this way: 14,014 kickoff returns, 4,999 punt returns, 2,336 receiving, and 1,967 rushing.

MOST ALL-PURPOSE YARDS, SEASON

Rank	Player	Team	Yards	Year
1.	DARREN SPROLES	SAINTS	2,696	2011
2.	DERRICK MASON	TITANS	2,690	2000
3.	MICHAEL LEWIS	SAINTS	2,647	2002
4.	LIONEL JAMES	CHARGERS	2,535	1985
5.	FRED JACKSON	BILLS	2,516	2009

▲ DARREN SPROLES

ONE-MAN SHOW

In a 1995 game, the Denver Broncos' Glyn Milburn ran the ball all over the field. He set a record that day with 404 all-purpose yards, including 133 yards on kickoff returns, 131 yards rushing, 95 yards on punt returns, and 45 yards receiving. He scored no touchdowns, however, and the Broncos could have used one. They lost to the Seahawks 31-27.

END-TO-END RECORDS

A football field is 100 yards long, goal line to goal line. With the 10-yard end zones, however, return plays (kickoffs, punts, and turnovers) can exceed 100 yards. Here are the longest return plays in NFL history:

KICKOFF RETURN: 109 yards, Cordarrelle Patterson, Minnesota Vikings (2013)

PUNT RETURN: 103 yards, Robert Bailey, Los Angeles Rams (1994)

INTERCEPTION RETURN: 107 yards, Ed Reed, Baltimore Ravens (2008)

FUMBLE RETURN: 104 yards, Jack Tatum, Oakland Raiders (1972), and Aeneas Williams, Arizona Cardinals (2000)

MISSED FIELD GOAL RETURN: 109 yards, Antonio Cromartie, San Diego Chargers (2007)

CHAPTER 5

KICKERS

Kickers sometimes get overlooked in football, but they are some of the most important players on the field. Often they are the highest-scoring players on their teams, and many big games get decided by field goals in the final moments. During his long NFL career, Adam Vinateieri has been Mr. Clutch, nailing two Super Bowl-winning field goals for the New England Patriots and making more playoff field goals than any other kicker.

Teams don't just want kickers with ice in their veins, unafraid of having the ball on their toes when the game's on the line. They want consistent, accurate kickers who put points on the board. Kickers' accuracy can be measured by success rate, or field-goal percentage. This stat reflects their made field goals divided by total attempts.

How much better are kickers getting? They kick much farther, more often, and more accurately today than in the past. In the 2013 season, NFL kickers made an all-time high 86.5 percent of their field goals. That included 96 of 143 (67.1 percent) at a distance of 50 or more yards. Twenty years earlier, kickers had a 76.6 percent overall success rate and were just 61 of 120 (50.8 percent) from 50 or more yards. In 1973 they made only 63.1 percent of their kicks, including 10 of 62 (16.1 percent) from long range.

CAREER FIELD GOAL PERCENTAGE

Rank	Player	Team	Field Goal %
1.	JUSTIN TUCKER	RAVENS	89.82%
2.	DAN BAILEY	COWBOYS	89.75%
3.	STEPHEN GOSTKOWSKI	PATRIOTS	86.79%
4.	MIKE VANDERJAGT	COLTS/COWBOYS	86.47%
5.	NATE KAEDING	CHARGERS/DOLPHINS	86.20%

◄ ADAM VINATIERI

PERFECTION
AND NEAR PERFECTION

Gary Anderson's perfect 1998 regular season for the Minnesota Vikings ended up not being so memorable. With 2:18 remaining in the NFC Championship Game following that season, he missed a 38-yard try that would have given the Vikings a 10-point lead. Instead the upset-minded Atlanta Falcons tied the game with a late touchdown. The Falcons went on to win in overtime and advanced to the Super Bowl.

In 2015 the NFL moved the line for the extra-point kick after a touchdown from the 2-yard line to the 15-yard line. Why? To make it a greater challenge for the game's expert kickers. A season earlier, kickers made 99.3 percent of their PATs (just eight misses in 1,143 tries). They were still pretty good from 32 yards (the new distance), making 93 percent of attempts in 2015 preseason games.

PERFECT SEASONS

Rank	Player	Team	Year	Field Goals
1.	MIKE VANDERJAGT	COLTS	2003	(37 OF 37)
2.	GARY ANDERSON	VIKINGS	1998	(35 OF 35)
3.	TONY ZENDEJAS	RAMS	1991	(17 OF 17)
	JEFF WILKINS	RAMS	2000	(17 OF 17)
5.	GARRETT HARTLEY	SAINTS	2008	(13 OF 13)
6.	SHAYNE GRAHAM	PATRIOTS	2010	(12 OF 12)

◀ GARY ANDERSON

SIDELINING THE KICKER

Football coaches and coordinators try to have a feel for the game as it goes on, calling plays based on their game plan and their gut. But are they taking the statistics into account?

One of the toughest decisions to make is whether to go for it on fourth down. Teams get four downs to gain 10 yards. Analysts have examined hundreds of games and plays to gauge the best times to take the chance, and they determined that coaches should do it much more than they do.

According to *The New York Times*' 4th Down Bot, teams should go for it on fourth and 1 almost every time, especially early in close games. They succeed more than they fail, the stats show.

▼ ARIZONA CARDINALS

FOURTH DOWN SUCCESS RATE, 2014

Rank	Team	Rate	%
1.	ARIZONA CARDINALS	3 OF 4	75%
2.	PHILADELPHIA EAGLES	7 OF 11	63.6%
3.	OAKLAND RAIDERS	9 OF 15	60%
	CAROLINA PANTHERS	6 OF 10	60%
5.	HOUSTON TEXANS	10 OF 17	58.8%

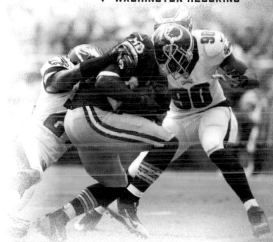

▼ WASHINGTON REDSKINS

For the Cardinals and Eagles, going for it paid off in 2014. They were successful on more than 60 percent of their fourth-down attempts. The Washington Redskins were the worst team on fourth down that season, going 4 of 16 for 25 percent.

RISKY BUSINESS

New England Patriots coach Bill Belichick isn't afraid to play the odds and go for it on fourth down. But one of his bold decisions blew up in his face. During a 2009 game against the rival Indianapolis Colts, the Patriots tried to seal a six-point win by running a fourth-down play. They were on their own 28-yard line, and about two minutes remained on the clock. The Colts made the stop and took advantage of the short field. The Colts quickly scored and won the game.

YOU MAKE THE CALL

During the NFC Championship Game following the 2014 season, the Green Bay Packers led the Seattle Seahawks 16-0 at halftime and 19-7 with less than five minutes remaining. The Seahawks rallied to force overtime and won the game 28-22 to advance to the Super Bowl. But did the Packers lose the game early on, even though they had a big lead? Twice they had fourth-and-goal plays from the 1-yard line, and head coach Mike McCarthy settled for field goals instead of trying for touchdowns.

Statistics measuring similar plays in previous seasons showed NFL teams scored on such attempts a bit more than half of the time. According to those stats, teams have a 55-percent chance of scoring touchdowns on those plays. Other stats show that 2014 Seahawks' opponents had converted 8 of 14 fourth-down plays, or 57 percent. The stats seem to say the Packers should have gone for it. On the other hand, the game was in Seattle's CenturyLink Field, the NFL's loudest outdoor stadium. Also, the Seahawks had the NFL's best defense. A goal-line stand by the home team would have fired up the crowd and might have changed the momentum.

What do you think? Did McCarthy make the right calls?

A SURE THING?

Field goal distance is measured from the spot of the kick, which is about seven yards behind the line of scrimmage, to the goalpost, which is located at the back of the 10-yard end zone. That adds about 17 yards to the line of scrimmage. In 2014 NFL kickers were perfect on 10 field goals of 19 yards and under, and they made 241 of 247 kicks—97.6 percent—from 29 yards and closer. The last time an NFL kicker missed a chip shot after his team stalled at the 1- or 2-yard line was in 2002.

SCORING

- Touchdown, 6 points
- PAT (point after touchdown), 1 point (kick) or 2 points (run or pass)
- Field goal, 3 points
- Safety, 2 points

▶ SHANE LECHLER

Punters have an important job. When their teams get stuck out of field goal range on fourth down, punters play a crucial role. It's up to them to keep field position to their advantage. They must kick the ball away and pin their opponents deep in their own territory.

Punts are measured by distance from the line of scrimmage to the point where the ball is caught, goes out of bounds, is declared dead and downed, or at the goal line in the case of a touchback. That's the gross yardage. Net yardage is also measured. Net yardage takes into account return yards or subtracts 20 yards in the case of a touchback.

Shane Lechler of the Oakland Raiders and Houston Texans owns the best gross yardage average for a career. In his first 15 seasons, he booted balls an average of 47.5 yards per punt.

In the 2009 season, Lechler's average punt went 51.1 yards. The only player with a higher single-season average was Hall-of-Fame quarterback Sammy Baugh of the Washington Redskins. In 1940, before punters were specialists, "Slinging Sammy" averaged 51.4 yards per punt.

TOP YARDS-PER-PUNT AVERAGE, CAREER

Rank	Player	Team	Yards-per-Punt
1.	SHANE LECHLER	RAIDERS/TEXANS	47.5
2.	BRYAN ANGER	JAGUARS	47.0
	THOMAS MORSTEAD	SAINTS	47.0
4.	BRANDON FIELDS	DOLPHINS	46.8
5.	ANDY LEE	49ERS	46.2

INSIDE JOB

Punters try to accomplish two tasks with their kicks: They want to get good distance as well as good hang time—the number of seconds the ball travels through the air. The hope is that the distance will pin the opposing team deep in its own territory. Good hang time allows defenders enough time to dash down field to make tackles. Punters also hope to avoid touchbacks, which allow teams to begin offensive drives at the 20-yard line. The NFL keeps track of punts hit inside the 20. In 2014 the Philadelphia Eagles' Donnie Jones and the Arizona Cardinals' Drew Butler each landed 34 (of 76 and 79 punts, respectively) inside the 20, the most in the NFL.

As a general rule, punt returners waiting on the 10-yard line are supposed to let a punt fall behind them with the hope that it goes all the way to the end zone for a touchback. Still, there have been some players who have broken the rule and ended up with very long punt returns. In 1994 Robert Bailey of the Rams took the ball out of the end zone and dashed 103 yards for a touchdown. In 2001 Patrick Peterson of the Cardinals returned a punt 99 yards.

The shortest punt return for a touchdown in NFL history was 5 yards. In 1985 in Chicago, New York Giants punter Sean Landeta nearly missed the punt, and the ball dribbled off the side of his foot. The Bears' Shaun Gayle scooped it up at the 5-yard line and jogged to pay dirt.

◀ DREW BUTLER

Some of the longest punts in NFL history don't necessarily come from distance or hang time, but rather from some favorable bounces and rolls. Steve O'Neal's 98-yarder had a little of everything. With his team on its own 1-yard line, O'Neal's kick traveled nearly 75 yards in the air before bouncing and rolling to the opposite 1-yard line, where it was downed.

LONGEST PUNTS

Rank	Player	Team	Yards	Year
1.	STEVE O'NEAL	JETS	98	1969
2.	SHAWN MCCARTHY	PATRIOTS	93	1991
3.	RANDALL CUNNINGHAM	EAGLES	91	1989
4.	DON CHANDLER	PACKERS	90	1965
	RODNEY WILLIAMS	GIANTS	90	2001

CHAPTER 7
DEFENSE

The goal of the defense is simple: stop the opposing team from moving the ball and scoring. One of the best ways to do that is by tackling— bringing the player with the ball to the ground. A player's tackle total is a combination of solo tackles and assists. Assists are cases in which more than one player is involved in the tackle. For many years, tackles were an unofficial stat recorded by team statisticians. Now officials observing the game from the press box keep careful track of which defenders make the plays.

In 2014 Carolina Panthers linebacker Luke Kuechly led the NFL with 153 tackles. The total included 99 solo stops and 54 assists. The NFL's single-game record for tackles is 25 by Chicago Bears linebacker Brian Urlacher in 2006. Twelve of the 25 were solo tackles.

Tackles for loss are also tracked. Those are plays in which a defender brings down a ball carrier, other than a quarterback dropping back to pass, behind the line of scrimmage for negative yards. In 2013 St. Louis Rams defensive end Robert Quinn had 23 tackles for loss and 57 total tackles. A whopping 40.4 percent of his tackles took place behind the line of scrimmage.

LEADING TACKLERS, 2014

Rank	Player	Team	Tackles
1.	LUKE KUECHLY	PANTHERS	153
2.	DEANDRE LEVY	LIONS	151
3.	LAVONTE DAVID	BUCCANEERS	146
4.	CURTIS LOFTON	SAINTS	145
5.	PAUL WORRILOW	FALCONS	143

▶ LUKE KUECHLY

SACKED OUT

When a quarterback who is dropping back to pass is tackled, it is called a sack. Sacks are a separate category from tackles. When two players are involved in a sack, they split the stat, with the game's official scorers giving each credit for a half sack.

The sack wasn't introduced as an official stat until 1982. Although some of the game's best sack masters have played and set records since then, we don't really know who actually was history's best. Many believe the Rams' Deacon Jones may have compiled the most quarterback sacks. After all, he's the player who invented the term. But he played before officials tracked the stat.

▶ BRUCE SMITH

TOTAL SACKS, CAREER

Rank	Player	Team	Sacks
1.	BRUCE SMITH	BILLS/REDSKINS	200
2.	REGGIE WHITE	EAGLES/PACKERS/PANTHERS	198
3.	KEVIN GREEN	RAMS/STEELERS/PANTHERS/49ERS	160
4.	CHRIS DOLEMAN	VIKINGS/FALCONS/49ERS	150
5.	MICHAEL STRAHAN	GIANTS	141

◄ MICHAEL STRAHAN

Michael Strahan of the New York Giants holds the single-season record for sacks, bringing down quarterbacks 22 1/2 times in 2001. Since then two players have missed by a half sack: the Vikings' Jared Allen in 2011 and the Chiefs' Justin Houston in 2014.

SHUT IT DOWN

The best cornerbacks in the NFL aren't necessarily the ones who intercept the ball all the time. In fact, some of the best ones don't get many chances for a takeaway. Coaches study film and stats, and often they choose not to challenge so-called shutdown corners such as Richard Sherman or Darrelle Revis. By making that choice, they basically cut their playbook—and the football field—in half.

Quarterbacks challenged the Seahawks' Sherman just 65 times in 2014, although he was on the field for 552 passing plays. On all but 11.8 percent of the plays, Sherman didn't see the ball. Still he intercepted four passes and defended 12 that season. Revis, playing for the Patriots, was targeted 79 times in 606 passing plays (13 percent). The Patriots defeated the Seahawks in the Super Bowl that season.

At the other end of the spectrum, Jason McCourty of the Tennessee Titans was thrown at 125 times in 576 plays (21.7 percent). He had three interceptions and 14 defended passes. Clearly, quarterbacks were not afraid to throw to his side of the field.

► RICHARD SHERMAN

In 2014 J.J. Watt had one of the greatest seasons ever for a defensive player. Besides his 20 1/2 sacks and 29 tackles for loss, he defended 11 passes, batting down most of them at the line of scrimmage (hence the nickname J.J. Swat). He also forced four fumbles and ran one interception and one fumble recovery back for scores.

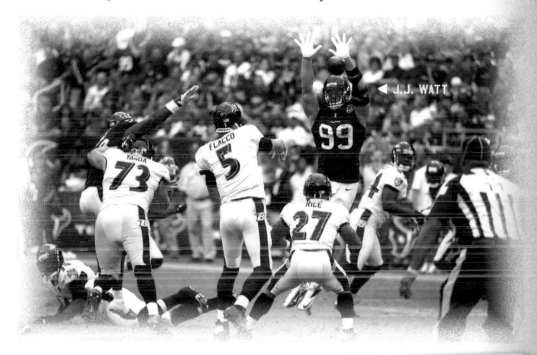

◄ J.J. WATT

TOTAL INTERCEPTIONS, CAREER

Rank	Player	Team	Interceptions
1.	PAUL KRAUSE	REDSKINS/VIKINGS	81
2.	EMLEN TUNNELL	GIANTS/PACKERS	79
3.	ROD WOODSON	STEELERS/49ERS/RAVENS/RAIDERS	71
4.	DICK LANE	RAMS/CARDINALS/LIONS	68
5.	KEN RILEY	BENGALS	65

STAT STARS

MOST POINTS IN A SEASON

LADAINIAN TOMLINSON, RB,
Chargers, 186 (2006)

MOST TOUCHDOWNS, ALL-TIME

JERRY RICE, WR,
49ers/Raiders/Seahawks, 208

▲ JERRY RICE

MOST TOUCHDOWNS, SINGLE GAME

GALE SAYERS, RB, **Bears, 6 (Dec. 12, 1965)**

MOST TOUCHDOWN PASSES, ALL-TIME

PEYTON MANNING, QB, **Colts/Broncos, 530**

MOST NON-OFFENSIVE TOUCHDOWNS

DEVIN HESTER, **Bears/Falcons, 20**

MOST INTERCEPTIONS IN A SEASON

DICK "NIGHT TRAIN" LANE, **Rams, 14 (1952)**

▲ PEYTON MANNING

MOST CAREER RUSHING YARDS

EMMITT SMITH, **Cowboys/Cardinals, 18,355**

MOST CAREER PASSING YARDS

BRETT FAVRE, QB, Falcons/Packers/Jets/Vikings, 71,838

MOST RUSHING YARDS PER GAME, CAREER

JIM BROWN, RB, Browns, 104.3

MOST RECEIVING YARDS PER GAME IN A SEASON

WES CHANDLER, WR, Chargers, 129 (1982)

▲ BRETT FAVRE

HIGHEST PERCENTAGE OF PASSES THROWN FOR TOUCHDOWNS

SID LUCKMAN, QB, Bears, 7.9%

MOST SACKS, SINGLE GAME

DERRICK THOMAS, LB, Chiefs, 7 (Nov. 11, 1990)

MOST GAMES PLAYED

MORTEN ANDERSEN, K, Saints/Falcons/Giants/Chiefs/Vikings, 382

MOST CHAMPIONSHIPS

GREEN BAY PACKERS, 13 (includes four Super Bowls)

MOST SUPER BOWL VICTORIES

PITTSBURGH STEELERS, 6

STAT GLOSSARY

all-purpose yards—the total number of rushing, receiving, and kick/punt return yards for a player

completion percentage—the percentage of a quarterback's passes that are caught by a teammate; receptions divided by total throws

field goal percentage—the percentage of successful field goal kicks; made field goals divided by total attempts

gross yardage (punting)—the number of yards a punted ball travels from the line of scrimmage to where it is caught, goes out of bounds, is declared dead and downed, or at the goal line in case of a touchback

net yardage (punting)—gross yards minus the number of yards a kick returner runs with the ball after catching it; in the case of a touchback, 20 yards are subtracted from the gross to get the net

passer rating—a complex formula used to determine a quarterback's or other passer's success throwing the ball

passes defended—defensive plays in which a pass is tipped, stripped, or batted away, preventing a catch

sack—the tackling of a quarterback behind the line of scrimmage as he is attempting a pass

tackle for loss—taking down a ball carrier behind the line of scrimmage, resulting in negative yards

touchdown-to-interception ratio—the number of touchdowns thrown by quarterback compared to the number of times he is intercepted

turnover—the offense's loss of the ball to the defense, usually by interception or fumble

yards after catch (YAC)—the number of yards a receiver runs with the ball after he has caught the pass

yards after contact—the number of yards a ball carrier runs with the ball after the first time he is touched by a defensive player

yards per attempt—the average number of yards gained on a play, which can be for a particular player, a position, or team; divide the total yards by the number of plays

READ MORE

The Editors of Sports Illustrated Kids. *Sports Illustrated Kids Big Book of Who: Football.* New York: Sports Illustrated, 2013.

Frederick, Shane. *Football: The Math of the Game.* North Mankato, Minn.: Capstone Press, 2012.

Hetrick, Hans. *Six Degrees of Peyton Manning: Connecting Football Stars.* North Mankato, Minn.: Capstone Press, 2015.

INTERNET SITES

FactHound offers a safe, fun way to find Internet sites related to this book. All of the sites on FactHound have been researched by our staff.

Here's all you do:

Visit *www.facthound.com*

Type in this code: 9781491482148

Super-cool stuff! Check out projects, games and lots more at **www.capstonekids.com**

INDEX